PREPARATION FOR SPECIAL
EDUCATION ADMINISTRATION

PREPARATION FOR SPECIAL EDUCATION ADMINISTRATION

By

GAIL A. HARRIS, Ed.D.

Independent Consultant
President, Harris Development Center
East Lansing, Michigan

CHARLES C THOMAS · PUBLISHER
Springfield · Illinois · U.S.A.

Published and Distributed Throughout the World by
CHARLES C THOMAS • PUBLISHER
Bannerstone House
301-327 East Lawrence Avenue, Springfield, Illinois, U.S.A.

© *1975, by* CHARLES C THOMAS • PUBLISHER
ISBN 0-398-03363-3
Library of Congress Catalog Card Number: 74-23875

With THOMAS BOOKS *careful attention is given to all details of*
manufacturing and design. It is the Publisher's desire to present books
that are satisfactory as to their physical qualities and artistic possibilities
and appropriate for their particular use. THOMAS BOOKS *will be true*
to those laws of quality that assure a good name and good will.

.

Printed in the United States of America
W-2

Library of Congress Cataloging in Publication Data

Harris, Gail A
    Preparation for special education administration.

    Includes index.
    1.   Mentally handicapped children—Education.
2.   Handicapped children—Education.   3.   School
administrators, Training of—Simulation methods.
I.   Title.
LC4602.H37   371.9'042   74-23875
ISBN 0-398-03363-3

PREFACE

T HIS BOOK CONTAINS simulation exercises based on the experiences of the author as a director of special education of a local school system. The exercises contain questions or requests which require a response on the part of the director of special education. They cover all or most of the areas which are included in a comprehensive special education program.

The exercises are assembled in the categories of Personnel, In-service Education and Consultation, Pupil-Personnel, Curriculum, Parents, Relationships with General Education, Board of Education, Relationships with Other Agencies, Community Resources, Committees and Public Relations, Transportation, Housing, Finances, Forms and Records, and General Principles. Each section contains a set of exercises followed by some suggested general guiding principles to help the user determine how to respond.

These simulation exercises are meant to serve as a tool in the practical preparation of special education administrators. Names are completely fictitious. Additional exercises may also be developed to add to each section.

It is hoped that this book will help prepare special education administrators to smoothly handle communications, develop the ability to obtain the facts, sift through various alternative responses, reflect on guiding philosophies and respond in an efficient and effective manner.

ACKNOWLEDGMENTS

MANY THANKS ARE extended to the agencies and individuals serving handicapped citizens in Michigan for providing me with the experiences which have led to the potential sharing of the contents of this book for instructional purposes. These professional experiences have included being an attendant nurse at a state institution for the mentally retarded, directing a summer playground program for the severely handicapped, teaching the trainable and educable mentally retarded at a state institution, teaching the educable retarded in a local school system, serving as a consultant for the state department of education, teaching at two universities, directing special projects for various agencies as an independent consultant and directing a local school system's special education program.

Special thanks are extended to the Michigan Association for Retarded Citizens for keeping me practical and empathetic to the needs of the handicapped and their parents.

GAIL A. HARRIS

CONTENTS

PREPARATION FOR SPECIAL
EDUCATION ADMINISTRATION

Chapter 1

THE SETTING

T HE SETTING IS Hazelwood School District, which has a school membership of almost 10,000 pupils. It is the only school district in the city of Hazelwood, which is a suburb of one of the nation's largest cities.

You are the Director of Special Education. Other central office administrative staff for the school district includes the Superintendent, Dr. Goodenough; the Deputy Superintendent, Dr. Paulson; the Assistant Superintendent, Dr. Newburg; the Community School Director, Mr. Keane; and the Director of Vocational Education, Mr. Hanks.

The population is primarily southern Appalachian white, whose occupations center around the auto industry.

The school buildings in Hazelwood are:

Building	Principal
High School	Mr. Proud
Garden Secondary	Mr. Biddle
Goodenough Junior High	Mr. Bell
Beecher Junior High	Mr. Horstman

Elementary Schools:

Clark	Mr. Mack
Edison	Mr. Gibbs
Ford	Mr. Williams
Hoover	Mr. Hilley
Longfellow	Mr. Angel
Roosevelt	Mr. Wood
United Oaks	Mrs. White

Wanda...........................Mr. Winans
Webster...........................Miss Long

The state law requiring or mandating special education provisions for the handicapped from zero to twenty-five years of age has just passed and will take effect in one year. However, the school district has always prided itself on its exemplary educational services for the handicapped, resulting in a large network of programs and services provided within the district to both public and parochial students, and also through cooperation with neighboring school districts.

Hazelwood has special education classroom programs which have a specially trained teacher serving a small number of students who have a similar handicap. Pupils are placed in special education classes within regular school buildings when they are unable to obtain maximum benefit from regular class placement and when they meet the criteria for eligibility for the specific special education program. They are placed in special education classes through the action of an educational planning and placement committee. Other students wtih handicaps may remain in a regular classroom, but require one or more special services.

The current provisions in Hazelwood for the handicapped include the following special education classroom programs.

Elementary Educable Mentally Retarded: with six classes in Webster School, serves educable mentally retarded from five to thirteen years of age. These students are usually at least two years behind academically, socially immature and have one-half to three-quarters as much intelligence (determined by psychological testing) as their normal peers.

Secondary Educable Mentally Retarded: with eleven classes in Garden School, serves educable mentally retarded from thirteen to twenty-one years of age. This is an extension of the elementary level program. Garden School also houses the Study and Vocational Skills (SAVS) program for potential drop-outs from school, serving pupils from thirteen to eighteen years of age. These pupils are identified by poor interpersonal and group social skills, disruptive classroom behavior, underachievement in terms of tested potential, reading difficulty, withdrawal from participation, predelinquent tendencies and a school history of repeated failures. The pupils in special education and in the SAVS program are integrated in classes.

Trainable Mentally Retarded: with one class in Ford School, serves trainable mentally retarded from five to fourteen years of age. These students are far behind academically, are socially immature, frequently have multiple handicaps (including physical and speech problems) and have one-third to one-half as much intelligence (determined by psychological testing) as their normal peers.

Orthopedically Handicapped: with two classrooms, plus a physical therapy room in Roosevelt School, serves the physically handicapped from six to twenty-five years of age. A physician provides written verification to the school district that the physical problems of the student require special educational placement. Physical therapy is provided by a specialist in this area, as directed by the physician for each student.

Adjusted Study Program: with two classes at Hoover School, serves emotionally disturbed pupils who have normal intelligence. School social worker service, psychological testing and a psychiatric evaluation are prerequisites for this program. The pupils served in this program are from six to thirteen years of age.

Perceptual Development Program: with two classes at Clark School, serves neurologically handicapped pupils from six to twelve years of age. Pupils with learning disabilities are placed in this program after comprehensive evaluation procedures. The students are of normal intelligence, are behind academically and have neurological deficits. They usually have poor gross or fine muscle coordination, are hyperactive, and have expressive or receptive language problems.

Preschool Language Development: with one half-day class at Edison School, serves pupils with severe language development problems from three to five years of age. Referrals to the program are made through the speech correctionist.

Preschool Multiple Handicapped Program: with two half-day classes at Edison School serves pupils with two or more significant handicaps from three to five years of age. Federally funded, it provides for preschool evaluation and instruction. Parental counseling is also provided for parents of handicapped children, from infancy to five years of age, through this program.

Special services are also available for handicapped pupils who are able to remain in the regular classroom. Hazelwood School District sponsors the following special services.

School Social Worker: helps pupils, school staff, parents and the community to identify adverse conditions, needed services and resources, to plan and execute the programs required for pupils who are socially maladjusted. The four school social workers in Hazelwood School District work primarily with individual pupils, utilizing the casework method. A male and female school social worker team up to work with one group of high school students, once weekly, for one hour at the high school.

Speech Correction: with six speech correctionists, serves students with speech and language problems. The correctionist works either individually or in small groups, seeing each student for thirty-minute periods twice weekly, in accordance with the state regulations covering this program. The types of cases vary, with about 90 percent of the caseload of seventy-five to one hundred pupils for each correctionist being defective articulation and the balance consisting of delayed speech, hearing problems, stuttering, voice problems, cleft palate, or language development problems.

Type C Teacher-Consultant: serves educable mentally handicapped pupils who are able to function in the regular grades with the special help of the teacher-consultant who visits twice weekly.

Teacher/Counselor for the Physically Handicapped: serves physically handicapped students in all grades who are able to function with special help in the regular grades. The caseload includes students who are blind, partially sighted, hard of hearing, and orthopedically handicapped. Special adjustments in instructional equipment and supplies are provided in this program.

Teacher/Counselor for the Emotionally Disturbed: serves junior and senior high students who, because of emotional problems, require special counseling or tutorial services. Three staff members serve in this capacity, one in the high school and one in each of the two junior high schools.

Homebound Teacher: serves students who, because of a physical handicap, are expected to be confined to their home for six weeks or more. This program is sponsored by the neighboring school district of Fernwood, with one shared staff member.

School Psychologists: provide psychological testing of students referred to them due to learning problems. Hazelwood School District employs two school psychologists. In addition, the federal grant for the preschool project involves the services of a part-time consulting psychologist who serves that program.

Hazelwood School District also has two curriculum supervisors. The secondary supervisor, Mr. Biddle, serves as the principal of Garden School. The elementary supervisor, Mr. Foote, serves as curriculum leader for the elementary special education classroom programs.

Students with the following handicaps are taken by bus to special education classrooms in neighboring school districts: hearing impairments, vision impairments, and the older trainable mentally retarded pupils.

Outside consultants to the Hazelwood special education program include a psychiatrist one-half day per week, a psychologist for the preschool project and special in-service education speakers at regular intervals.

The county or intermediate school district supplements the local school district provisions with a reading clinic, homebound services, psychiatric evaluations, psychological evaluations, speech and hearing evaluations, and vocational rehabilitation consultations.

Further consultative resources are available through the state department of education which provides special education consultant services.

The community has the services also of the Youth Protection Agency (a precourt referral helping agency), the Child Guidance Clinic, the Community Mental Health Clinic, university speech and hearing clinics, and residential centers for the emotionally disturbed.

Some of the exercises in this book require an immediate, common sense response, while others should be handled by delegation to another person or agency, further research to obtain the necessary information, or committee assignment. They are all situations which a director of special education is likely to face.

Chapter 2

PERSONNEL

THE REQUESTS FOR ACTION

1. Betty Boyle has just graduated in special education and is interested in teaching in your system. She wants to know the process for applying and whether there are any vacancies.

2. Dave Jones, a sixth grade regular class teacher in your school system, wants to become a special education teacher. What do you advise him to do?

3. The university special education advisor wants to place three student teachers next term in your program at Hazelwood. What do you do about it?

4. A university student contacts you and reminds you that two terms ago, he did a project with special education students at your secondary vocational center. He now wants to student teach there. You recall that some questions were raised about his exceptionally chummy relationship with one of the male students. How do you respond?

5. Margaret Mackey asks about your need for a teacher's aide in one of the special education programs. She would like to visit the program to see if she might be interested, and to obtain

any written materials. What various responses regarding process and visit do you make?

6. Noona Eaton asks about the ad for a lunchroom supervisor for special education. She wants to know about the duties. Tell her.

7. The new secretary who handles substitute teachers calls to let you know that two special education teachers are out ill today, one an elementary classroom teacher, and the other a special service speech correctionist. How do you handle both situations?

8. A special education teacher from a neighboring district asks you about possible employment in your summer program. She wants to know what you will be offering and what your priorities are in hiring staff.

9. After the principal of an elementary school tells you that a speech correctionist has been out for three days without notifying her building, you call the correctionist at home. She tells you she has been having car troubles. What do you do?

10. A teacher aide in a program for the emotionally disturbed calls in the evening to tell you that some parents of a child she hit with a toilet bowl brush during the day are upset because the girl came home with brush welts on her legs. She says they'll probably call you soon. What do you say to the teacher aide?

11. The teachers' union representative wants to discuss your excessive calling of after-school meetings as reported to him by one of your teachers. He also wants to discuss the small number

of psychological tests completed by one of the school psychologists. How do you prepare for the meeting with him?

12. The university inquires if you have any teachers with high potential for success in a doctoral program, who might be interested in a year's leave from Hazelwood, with a scholarship to attend the university full-time. What efforts do you make to respond?

13. Mr. Foote, the special education curriculum supervisor, expresses concern over a teacher's management of her pupils, noting that he has already discussed this twice with the teacher with no results. What additional information do you request, how do you advise Mr. Foote, and what action do you take?

14. Two elementary special education teachers contact you to indicate dissatisfaction with the special education curriculum supervisor, Mr. Foote. They state he is not effective in providing assistance and spends about one hour per day in the special education shop making items for his personal use and as Christmas gifts for his relatives. What do you do?

15. The parochial school principal comments on the improved services from the speech correctionist whom you have assigned to provide assistance to that school. How do you respond?

16. In the summer, before school starts, you need to develop a letter to special education and special services staff with information regarding the new school year. What information should be included?

17. Dr. Goodenough, the superintendent, asks you to write a role description for a new elementary special education super-

visor position, to be presented to the board of education and to go to all staff members. Develop this role description.

18. You are planning the first fall special education staff meeting. What should be on the agenda?

19. A retired high school teacher from Hazelwood tells you she is interested in volunteering with the emotionally disturbed program. How do you respond and what steps do you take if you accept this volunteer service?

20. The elementary special education supervisor tells you that the Perceptual Development Program teacher aide will be absent one day. He asks if they will need a substitute teacher aide. If so, who should be the substitute? What should be done?

21. A teacher aide wants three days funeral leave with pay, since her father-in-law died and the service is in another state. She also asks if a substitute teacher aide can be employed while she is gone. How do you respond?

22. Linda Early, who handles teachers' sick calls and arranges for substitutes, wants to know who to inform when special service personnel, such as speech correctionists, are out.

23. There are two psychologists in Hazelwood School District's special education program. One has a Ph.D. and asks to be named coordinator of psychological services. What do you do?

24. You are to interview candidates for the following positions: elementary educable mentally retarded, secondary educable mentally retarded, elementary emotionally disturbed, and speech correction. Would you handle the interviews differently? What information would you share with them? Hold a mock interview for each position.

25. A parochial school principal complains that the speech correctionist assigned to her building frequently arrives late and leaves early. What action should be taken?

26. One of your speech correctionists says he may be out a week with a kidney infection. Should a substitute be employed?

27. Mr. Gibbs, the principal of Edison Elementary School, complains that the school psychologist assigned to his building has not entered the building for two months. What do you tell him?

28. You are developing a staff newsletter. What topics might be included?

29. Superintendent Goodenough asks you what your policy is on teacher evaluation for nontenure and tenure teachers in both special education and special service areas. What is it?

30. Mr. Biddle, the secondary special education building principal, reports he suspects two male teachers of "extra-sexual" activity. He also reports one of the teachers took a boy in his room (according to student reports), turned the lights out and locked the door. The students outside heard scuffling and laughing. The boy involved later had a welt on his arm and a bump on his head. What do you do?

31. Mr. Biddle, principal of Garden School, reports that two parents have complained that a teacher is physically torturing their sons. What actions should be taken?

32. Mr. Biddle, principal of Garden School, and you, have agreed that the teacher in charge of operating the sheltered

workshop activities room is not effectively obtaining subcontract work, and the total program is less than successful. You both feel the teacher should be reassigned to Biology for next year. Mr. Biddle asks you to tell the teacher before the year end teachers' meeting next week. How do you handle this?

SUGGESTED GUIDELINES FOR ACTIONS

1. Regular positive communication should be maintained with the personnel involved in your program.

2. Personnel should be consulted about program needs and urged to provide leadership in the program.

3. There should be written policies regarding basic procedures such as reporting staff absences.

4. Respond promptly and efficiently to requests, and refer to other resources when appropriate. Do not handle matters that others have been assigned to handle.

5. Be well informed about teacher certification and special education approval processes in your state.

6. Get to know your teacher union representative on a friendly, positive basis.

7. Thoroughly know the details of your school system's master teacher contract.

8. Respond so that the dignity of all individuals concerned is maintained.

9. Potential new employees should be encouraged to visit the program considered.

10. Utilize the general education system whenever possible, such as in reporting teacher absences.

11. Involve the building principal and the special education teachers in the selection of employees related to their program.

12. Keep as your highest priority the provision of an exceptional program for the students.

13. Make every effort to keep teacher morale high, such as by repeating compliments about them when you receive them.

14. Get the facts in the total situation before you take decisive actions.

15. Meet face to face whenever possible, rather than depending on written communications.

16. Newsletters should provide important information of general interest to all receiving personnel. "Fillers" should not be required. Newsletters or memos should be periodically released.

17. A role description should contain specific guidelines regarding role expectations, plus a general catchall category of duties as assigned by the director of special education.

18. Volunteer services should have a specific job to do, well defined and developed by the building personnel.

19. There should be a policy regarding the employment of substitutes for the various positions. For instance, the policy quite likely would be not to employ a substitute for a short term absence of a special service person, such as a speech correctionist.

20. Make sure the call-in person for absent personnel has a schedule for special service personnel, so the appropriate building may be notified.

21. When a special service is large enough to need individual coordination apart from the total special education program, then a coordinator of that discipline may be named.

22. Complaints and compliments should be handled first between the parties involved.

23. Special education teacher evaluations should follow the same pattern as regular teacher evaluations, wherever possible. The building principal should evaluate the special education classroom teachers in his building.

24. Serious complaints regarding teachers require definitive action with the full knowledge of the director of special education. If possible, a written, signed statement from parents, specifying the exact nature of the complaint is helpful, particularly in the case of tenure teachers.

25. A different trial assignment for a teacher who is not functioning well in a particular course situation should be made, after attempts to evaluate and improve the teacher have been made.

26. Learn who the good substitute teachers are and hire them.

27. Help teachers get proper certification and approval.

28. Hire only the most capable personnel.

29. When hiring teachers, get a "letter of intent" to take the courses needed for approval from the teacher. Also, obtain a university statement indicating the courses the teacher needs for approval. Have the school issue a letter of intent to employ when the courses needed are completed.

Chapter 3

IN-SERVICE EDUCATION AND CONSULTATION

THE REQUESTS FOR ACTION

1. There are several new staff members in special education and special services who should have some orientation to the total system and to the specific programs they are in. Map out a plan to accomplish this.

2. The new federal project, "Preschool Program for the Multiply Handicapped" includes provisions for an outside consultant to be involved in testing, parental meetings and some in-service education programs for staff. There are funds to employ such a person two full days a month. How would you develop a plan to utilize the services of this outside consultant?

3. The university coordinator for regular student teachers in your school system wants you to speak at the regular meeting of the student teachers regarding "Special Services," including what they do for the teacher and students, and how to refer students. Develop such a presentation.

4. Mrs. White, the United Oaks principal, asks you to serve on a PTA panel with the school social worker and psychologist assigned to the building to discuss special services with the

parents. What information should the three of you include in the presentations.

5. Mr. Angel, the Longfellow principal, indicates he is to obtain a speaker for the state Association for Supervision and Curriculum Development meeting on the topic "Trends in Special Education." What else do you need to find out from him and to what resources could you refer him?

6. The state association president of administrators of special education invites you to chair that group's legislative committee and to suggest committee membership. How would you determine membership (size and members), and what would be your agenda for the first meeting of the committee? What information should you request from the president to help your committee develop most effectively?

7. An elementary principal asks about obtaining a special education consultant from the intermediate school district for a teachers' in-service education meeting. How will this be accomplished?

8. Mr. Mack, the principal at Clark School, asks you to arrange a half-day teacher workshop on special education instructional techniques. The workshop is to be held two weeks from now. What process would you use to develop this?

9. Mr. Mack asks if on the day of his half-day workshop the classes should be dismissed, or are substitute teachers needed. What do you tell him?

10. The State Council for Exceptional Children president asks you to chair a repeated ninety minute session at the state conference. What information do you need from him?

11. One of your elementary special education teachers of the mentally retarded has been invited to serve as a resource person at a state conference for persons in comparable positions, and she asks your permission to accept. What is your response?

12. The teacher-counselor for the physically handicapped asks permission to attend a three day state conference in a city 160 miles away. She has already attended several out of district meetings this year. What is your response?

13. The teacher aide for the emotionally disturbed requests paid time for one-half day to visit a mental health program. How would you respond and what factors do you consider?

14. A state department of education consultant informs you of a five day summer institute at the university on "Behavior Patterns of EMR Urban Youth." The stipend is seventy-five dollars. The institute is aimed at directors, supervisors, psychologists and social workers. You are invited to select one staff member to attend. What is your selection process?

15. You are concerned that your special service staff is not making adequate use of community and state resource agencies, especially in appropriate pupil referrals; such as state institutions, vocational rehabilitation services, community mental health services, and speech clinics. How do you proceed to remedy this?

16. Mr. Biddle, the Garden School principal, indicates the curriculum guide needs massive revision. What arrangements can be made to accomplish this?

17. You notice that one of the four school social workers is handling his paper work during a consulting session with the psychiatrist, and also places one phone call during the discussion

session. The sessions occur in the school social workers' office. How do you respond to this situation?

18. You have funds to employ an outside four person consultant team to evaluate your special education program. How do you determine the composition of the team and the areas you want evaluated?

19. The four man consultant team which has evaluated your special education program has submitted a written report. What do you do with this report?

20. You need to develop some in-service education programs aimed at the demands of special education teachers for tranquilizing medications for their pupils, beyond that recommended by the physicians. Who would you involve as resources and how would you accomplish this in-service education?

SUGGESTED GUIDELINES FOR ACTIONS

1. Learning is enhanced by actually seeing or doing, rather than by complete dependence on the spoken word.

2. New programs sponsored by federal grants should fit into the total system and receive the same opportunities for special services as other programs. They may be considered as supplements to the current system of services.

3. Clearly spell out, at the beginning of the agreement, exactly what is expected of an outside consultant.

4. Utilize an outside consultant to provide services which the regular staff may not have the time, skill, or objectivity to perform.

5. In developing a public presentation, put yourself in the shoes of the listener to help determine what the presentation should include.

6. Resources for speaking engagements may help to be

determined on the basis of topic to be discussed, nature and size of audience, funds (if any) available, length of desired presentation and other affecting factors. Broad consideration of all resources (local, state and national) may then be on the basis of who can best do the job.

7. Establish clear ground rules for the operation of a committee. These ground rules should include at least the following: purpose of committee, lifetime of committee, communication channels, funds available, secretarial services, reporting schedule, and any authorization to expand membership if necessary.

8. Keep committee membership small.

9. Assist principals in providing in-service education programs about special education and special services, including contacting the speakers.

10. The building teachers should be involved in planning in-service education programs.

11. The master teacher contract should spell out the provisions for counting in-service education days. If in doubt, confer with the superintendent or other administrator in charge of regular in-service education.

12. Encourage your staff members to participate in leadership capacities, as it helps them grow in professional stature and also improves the image of your program.

13. Have a policy on conference attendance, including a total maximum number of days allowed per professional.

14. Involve teachers in the development of written curriculum guides.

15. Make use of special grant requests for summer projects for teachers, such as the revision of curriculum guides.

16. Utilize university consultant resources in helping to improve curriculum.

17. Outside consultants should be provided a room in which the participants are not tempted to divide their attention.

18. The recommendations in evaluation reports should be carefully reviewed and a follow up practical implementation plan developed with provision for periodic re-evaluation.

19. Involve specialists in in-service education programs with specific expertise in the target area of discussion.

Chapter 4

PUPIL PERSONNEL

THE REQUESTS FOR ACTION

1. Mr. Winans, the Wanda School principal, asks you what to do with a new boy whose mother said he was "under psychiatric care." What do you tell him?

2. The public health nurse informs you that a special private clinic research day school is referring, for public school special education placement, a ten year old autistic boy from your school district. He sits, waves his fingers in front of his eyes, and doesn't communicate other than with groans. What process do you suggest?

3. Mr. Hilley, the Hoover School principal, wants a child tested before talking with the parents, since they are "always uncooperative." Your policy is to always obtain the permission of the parents before psychological testing. How do you react?

4. One of the school social workers, Mrs. Cohen, has conferred with the psychiatrist who evaluated a boy and says he urgently needs placement in a class for the emotionally disturbed; however the written psychiatric report will not be received for two weeks. Mrs. Cohen wants to place him in the special education program immediately. How do you handle this?

5. The public health nurse has discovered a four year old with a cleft palate and harelip, and is requesting a speech program. Indicate your procedure for handling this.

6. The public health nurse indicates she has referred a deaf student to the state school for the deaf for a two week intensive hearing evaluation, and asks that the school follow up. What do you need to do?

7. The psychologist indicates she believes a student she tested may have an organic impairment and should have a neurological evaluation. She wants to know who should handle such a referral.

8. A neurologist calls regarding a child who was referred from your school system for a neurological evaluation to see if he qualifies for a special education program. He asks you to tell him what specific type of information you need from him.

9. Mrs. Martin, a mother from the neighboring school district, says she has a five year old cerebral palsied daughter who has been attending a cerebral palsy clinic nursery school, but she would now like her enrolled in your orthopedic program. What process do you suggest she follow?

10. Mr. Hilley, the Hoover principal, informs you he has twins in his area who are five years ten months, both with an I.Q. of seventy-two, who have been in Head Start and kindergarten. He wonders about their next placement. What additional information do you need, and what would be your process for handling the situation up to the moment of some placement.

11. Mr. Hartman, a father from a neighboring school district,

says he is moving to your district during the middle of the year. He has a ten year old retarded son who is in special education, and he would like him to remain in his current classroom at least for the rest of this year, if possible. He says he will transport him daily if it is necessary. What arrangements will you make and with whom?

12. Mr. Horstman, the principal of Beecher Junior High, informs you that two neighborhood boys (twenty-year-old twins) roam all day and peer in the school windows. He says they were in trainable classes. He would like to see them appropriately occupied during the day and asks for your help in getting this done. How do you proceed to accomplish this?

13. The junior high assistant principal reports an eighth grade girl is telling other girls that her twenty-one-year-old brother is having sexual relations with her, and the girl is showing others lewd pictures of herself with an older neighborhood man. He asks you what he should do. What do you tell him?

14. Mr. Hilley, the Hoover principal, says he has just found a five-year-old who weighs fifty-six pounds, is forty-six inches tall, acts like a three year old and is not in school. The mother says he was brain damaged at birth, which caused a speech problem, and he wets the bed each night. The principal asks for directions for handling this problem.

15. A grandmother expresses concern about her three-year-old granddaughter who is not talking. Both parents were in special education classes for the retarded. How do you respond?

16. A community school agent from one of the elementary schools has found a nine-year-old boy who is paralyzed from the waist down, has never been in school and has not seen a physician

in five years. Both parents work different shifts. What are the next steps and by whom?

17. The attendance officer informs you of a new family with a twelve-year-old retarded boy who is not in school. The officer asks you to stop at the boy's house. What do you do when you stop at the house?

18. The United Cerebral Palsy Association Clinic has a cerebral palsied boy from Hazelwood in nursery school, whom they would like to place in regular kindergarten. What arrangements should you make and what information do you need?

19. The intermediate school district homebound teacher informs you she is serving, via phone hook up, an eighteen-year-old boy from your area with brain damage, severe motor impairment (with speech and vision affected), but with apparently at least average intelligence. She suggests the need for a referral to vocational rehabilitation. How do you proceed with this?

20. Miss Long, the Webster principal, contacts you about a nine-year-old boy from a regular grade who "has seen a psychiatrist, doesn't do his schoolwork, undressed once in the school yard and set a fire at home." She wants to know where to refer him.

21. A lady calls about her five- and one-half-year-old grandson who cannot talk or hear and had one eye punctured with a pin. She wants help for him. He is not in school. Map out a plan of action.

22. The court social worker asks for help regarding a fifteen year old fatherless boy, with a weak mother who provides no

guidance. The boy is a glue sniffer, has been truant from school
for five weeks, and the social worker feels that incarceration is
not the answer for him. What do you think should be done next?

23. A psychiatrist who has a strong attachment for a fifteen-
year-old boy (the boy stays at his home part of the time) indicates
that the special education shop teacher is "pressuring" his client.
How do you respond to the psychiatrist?

24. Superintendent Goodenough tells you that some parents
of a sixteen-year-old high school boy have shared their concerns
with him. The boy has "poor school attendance, is belligerent,
a loner, difficult to manage, cries, dislikes school and wants a
doctor." What action should you take?

25. The high school has a student who will be in a cast at
home for at least six weeks. Homebound teaching services will
be provided by the homebound teacher. What other activities
might you suggest to help the boy?

26. On Monday, the attendance officer informs you that two
girls (one junior high and one senior high) attempted suicide
over the weekend. He also notes that sixteen students have
venereal disease. What is your response to both these situations?

27. One of the school social workers, Mrs. Roberts, inquires
about what reports should be sent to the principal and to the
director of special education, before screening; in the case of
students referred to the program for the emotionally disturbed.
Referring to the state rules for program eligibility, and perhaps
supplemented by your own requirements; what reports are
necessary?

28. Mr. Biddle, the Garden School principal, has just dis-

covered that a student has stolen the master key to the lockers. Some things have been taken from the lockers. The student is always causing trouble and the parents always defend him. The principal wants to file a court petition and suspend the student. How do you respond to this?

29. The junior high counselor calls to ask permission to place a fourteen-year-old boy on half-days. (The approval of any plan to place any student on less than full day placement has been assigned by the superintendent to you.) The boy has an I.Q. of seventy-five, works at the fourth grade level and gets C's and D's on his report card. His family are "law breakers." The boy is very sophisticated, drinks and is the center of school drug activity, according to the counselor. What various responses could you make?

30. One of the speech correctionists, Mr. Browning, has found a thirty-year-old in the community with a severe speech problem. Even though the maximum age for school special education services is twenty-five years, Mr. Browning wants to take the case for the summer since he has some vacancies, and then plan to refer later to the university speech clinic. Do you approve?

31. Mrs. O'Berry, a special education teacher at Garden School, calls in horror to report one of her students who is retarded and disturbed, stares at her constantly, and today said: "I'd like to murder you." What action(s) should be taken?

32. Miss Rose, the teacher of the trainable retarded, asks if she has the right to exclude a troublesome twelve year old girl from school. What laws and regulations apply and how do you respond?

33. Miss Finney, the teacher in the Title Six pre-school pro-

gram for the multiply handicapped, says one of her mothers wants to place her child in the state institution for the mentally retarded. She wants to know who to contact. Is there a community representative for the institution in your area?

34. You have just employed a part-time social worker for the Title Six preschool program. Her task is to obtain developmental histories on all of the children referred to the project. What information do you want on the developmental history form and who should be involved in developing the form?

35. Mr. Carew, the teacher of the elementary class for the emotionally disturbed, has a very disruptive student for whom residential placement has been recommended. He wants to know what to do while the boy is awaiting residential placement. What are the options?

36. Mrs. Roberts, school social worker, is concerned about a recent December visit to the fatherless home of a five year old special education student. They needed groceries and will have little Christmas unless assistance is received. What resources do you suggest she contact?

37. An elementary special education teacher has learned that one of her families is moving to another state. She wants to know what to have the parents do to assure the placement of their retarded child in an appropriate program. What do you tell her?

38. You will have an annual year end total special education pupil evaluation to determine class assignments for next year. How should this be organized and who should be involved. Plan for both resident and nonresident pupils.

SUGGESTED GUIDELINES FOR ACTIONS

1. Obtain release of information forms to obtain evaluation reports on new pupils.

2. Obtain evaluation reports and past school records before special placement decisions are made.

3. Remember, special education is not the only answer to every school problem.

4. Whenever possible, arrange for a personal observation in the current school setting of a new referral.

5. Always inform the parents if special psychological testing is to occur. Obtain their signed permission.

6. Immediately, or as soon as possible, confer with the parents to share the results of special testing.

7. Sometimes a different staff member will be more effective in dealing with parents who appear uncooperative.

8. Determine reasons for "uncooperativeness" of the parents.

9. Consider trial placements in the special education classrooms to help determine the appropriateness of the group setting.

10. Develop a referral system for outside evaluations. For instance, public health nurses may be asked to assume the responsibility for referrals to physicians.

11. Have written material regarding criteria for entrance into a special education program or service.

12. Referrals from other school districts should go through the office of the director of special education from the other district.

13. Seriously handicapped individuals will need to have postschool plans made for programs and services from appropriate agencies. There should be a system to assure that this occurs.

14. Be aware of what is normal and abnormal behavior and what is somewhere in between and requires intervention other than special services.

15. Try regular class placement to determine if this might be appropriate whenever feasible.

16. Make sure that all school personnel are aware of special education and are referring appropriate pupils to the programs.

17. Assign a case manager to each pupil case to follow through with referrals, family contacts, etc.

18. Know the state rules and regulations for pupil eligibility for each special education or special service program.

19. A little flexibility in providing services to community residents is sometimes a practical, humanitarian approach. Trial services, such as speech evaluation for older residents, may lead to referrals to the most appropriate resources.

20. Be sure to give teachers direction as to specific information needed to evaluate class placements for next year.

21. Invite other special education directors to attend evaluations for the pupils from their districts who are in your special education programs.

22. Be sure to give a person the responsibility for follow up on needed referrals.

23. Release of information forms may be signed by the family before they move, thus hastening the transfer of records process.

24. Make maximum use of all community agencies in serving pupils and their families.

Chapter 5

CURRICULUM

THE REQUESTS FOR ACTION

1. You are beginning a program for six- to ten-year-old neurologically handicapped children. You and the teacher, Mrs. Thompson, are telling the Administrative Council about the program and what will be the specialized curriculum. What curriculum content do you tell them about? What do you say will be special about the program?

2. You and Mrs. Thompson, the new teacher of the program for the neurologically or perceptually handicapped, are developing an order for the new room for supplies and equipment. You only have desks, bulletin boards and blackboards in the room. What else would you need for these six- to ten-year-old pupils? How would you suggest the teacher obtain information about what to order?

3. Mr. Carew, the teacher of the elementary classroom for the emotionally disturbed, submits an order for ten BB guns, one for each of his pupils. You ask him the curriculum purpose, and he indicates it will teach a leisure skill, and give him the opportunity to instruct the pupils to use discipline with a weapon. Do you approve the order? Why or why not?

4. An elementary community school agent tells you a man

has been observed for three or four days cruising in a car near the elementary school at dismissal time. Yesterday he approached a girl, but was deterred by another car. The police have been notified, but the community school agent suggests the teachers should include curriculum information regarding this situation. How would you handle this?

5. The mother of an eight-year-old severely physically and mentally handicapped wheelchair bound boy complains that she wants more than "therapy" for her son. He is scheduled to attend the program for the orthopedically handicapped only one and one-half hours daily, and during this time he has two sessions. One session is physical therapy and the other is speech correction. How would you follow up on this communication.

6. Mr. Biddle, the Garden School principal, inquires about starting cosmetology classes and wants to know the requirements plus your general reaction to adding this to the curriculum. What else would you need to find out, and how do you respond?

7. Garden School wants to start a work placement program in the community for the retarded students. What outside resources might be called in?

8. Dr. Paulsen, the school business manager, wants the secondary special education summer students to work on the renovation of a barn on the school farm which is forty miles from Hazelwood. You refer the proposal to the summer planning committee and tell them you need what program and cost factor information?

9. You need to appoint a committee plus a chairman to plan the summer special education program. Who would you appoint?

10. The summer special education program planning committee chairman asks about the possibility of scheduling swimming regularly in one of the two junior high swimming pools. How should this be checked out?

11. Mr. Frederick, a speech correctionist, asks if they should accept nonresident pupils in the summer speech program. Should they?

12. Mr. Cook, a speech correctionist, asks if they should serve the trainable retarded during the regular school year. Should they?

13. The executive director of the county association for retarded citizens, wants to sponsor a recreation night once a week for the educable mentally retarded at Garden School with teacher cooperation. He suggests one parent volunteer each time, plus one volunteer from the school. How would you proceed with this request?

14. It is time to evaluate the total special education and special service programs. What factors for evaluation would you include and who would you involve?

15. The secondary special education program curriculum guide needs extensive revision. What procedures do you set in motion to accomplish this?

16. The elementary level teachers of the educable mentally retarded are dissatisfied with their reading textbooks and want to adopt a different basic text which would be followed throughout this special education program. What steps should be taken and how would the elementary principal be involved?

17. Because the two classes for the orthopedically handicapped include wide age and ability ranges, the teachers are requesting a teacher's aide to assist them on a shared basis. What assignments may properly be given to the teacher's aide?

18. A parent has shared a concern with you that the trainable mentally retarded curriculum is based too much on academics, to the exclusion of some practical information, such as learning to tie shoelaces, and field trip experiences. What do you suggest the parent do about this concern? What do you do about it?

19. You are concerned about the curriculum when substitute teachers are involved and decide to ask each teacher to compile a folder. The folder should be kept up to date. Submit in detail your request to the teachers to accomplish the above.

20. A university graduate student proposes to do a follow-up study of your educable mentally retarded graduates, to determine where they feel the special education curriculum could have been improved. He plans a personal interview with a written interview guide. He asks what specific items you would like on the interview questions. What do you tell him?

SUGGESTED GUIDELINES FOR ACTIONS

1. Many persons, including parents and students, have worthwhile suggestions to make regarding needed curriculum content and should be given an opportunity to share their ideas regularly.

2. Special education pupils deserve the same opportunities for special services, such as speech correction, as other pupils.

3. Programs should be evaluated periodically.

4. Outside consultants have an objective viewpoint to offer and should be involved in program evaluations, and also in general consultation.

5. Teachers who will be involved in implementing the curriculum should be involved in curriculum development.

6. Remember the special resources available to you in accomplishing objectives, such as grant money potential to sponsor a summer workshop on curriculum development.

7. Remember to utilize the nonsupervisory curriculum consultants available to you from the intermediate or county school district, and the state education agency.

8. Keep a petty cash account, so teachers may make small periodic purchases to meet classroom needs.

9. Do not hesitate to deny an order, if you feel its instructional value is highly questionable, or if it is inappropriate for the specific group.

10. Demand an adequate budget for needed supplies and equipment for staff.

11. Individual program plans with specific short and long range goals should be developed.

12. Encourage the involvement of community resources wherever appropriate in the special education curriculum.

13. Develop specific criteria for program evaluation.

14. Provide for communication to help coordinate the curriculum between the elementary and secondary portions of the special education program.

15. Arrange for parents to directly discuss their curriculum concerns with the teachers.

16. Give teachers time to work on curriculum by having half-days free periodically or by hiring substitute teachers.

Chapter 6

PARENTS

THE REQUESTS FOR ACTION

1. A mother calls to request psychological testing and a program for her six-year-old daughter who was in kindergarten one month last year and then sent home for the year. The daughter, Susie, has a cleft palate, is immature, is receiving speech therapy and has some hearing loss. She is also on tranquilizers. Indicate the additional information needed and directions regarding the next steps.

2. Mr. Winans, the Wanda School principal, tells you a parent has requested a copy of her child's psychological evaluation report for her doctor, since the doctor is considering prescribing a tranquilizer. The mother wants to take the report with her this week to the doctor. Do you approve of the principal giving her his copy, or do you suggest another procedure?

3. The parents of a special education student who was recently a traffic fatality want to establish a memorial fund for him at the school he attended. What procedures do you set in motion?

4. Mrs. Cranshaw, whose daughter Pam is waiting for placement for the summer only in a residential facility for the mentally retarded, says that the family can pay a maximum of one hundred twenty-five dollars out of the total three hundred dollar cost.

What resources should be explored, and by whom, for the extra costs?

5. Mrs. Barefoot called regarding her ten-year-old son, Sam, who is in a class for the educable mentally retarded. She claims the teacher made Sam walk home from school today. Mrs. Barefoot feels someone should have called her so she could have come after him. She is quite upset. How do you respond?

6. Mrs. Quin, the mother of a special education student, has children's clothing which she would like to donate to someone in need. Who should handle this?

7. Mr. Rowe contacts you to ask if his nineteen-year-old son can enter your special education secondary program. He says his son is "slightly retarded, but quite bright except for his speech." He dropped out of school at fourteen or fifteen years of age and has been at home since. Mr. Rowe would like him to receive vocational training. What will you do about this?

8. Mrs. Haskins calls to tell you her five-year-old daughter Brenda (a special education student in a class for perceptually handicapped) was sent home today and placed hereafter on a half-day schedule. She said the teacher said Brenda's tranquilizers are not strong enough. But her doctor says they are. What do you do about this?

9. You need to develop a letter to parents in the fall with information regarding the new school year, their child's placement, and other information. Develop the letter.

10. A lady tells you her four-year-old grandson and his parents will be moving into Hazelwood from Washington, D.C. She

suspects he is retarded and she knows he has been tested. What advice can you give her regarding appropriate action to take?

11. A distraught mother calls and tells you her son forgot his lunch when he got on the bus this morning, and she has no way to get it to him. How do you handle this if the school he is in has no hot lunch program?

12. You and the teacher are making a visit to the home of an eleven-year-old boy who has behavior problems, low school achievement and reportedly receives little affection at home. The purpose of the home visit is to report the boy's progress and spell out how the parents can help. What do you tell the parents?

13. One of the elementary principals reports he has a special education student with a bruise on his face which he believes is caused by parental abuse. What is the law in your state, or in your school system, regarding reporting child abuse cases?

14. A sobbing mother calls on Monday morning and tells you her sixteen year old mentally retarded daughter and her girl-friend were taken by a special education classmate and his father to a motel room on the weekend. Both girls had sexual intercourse with the father and the son. She has called the police and wonders what else she should do. What laws regarding this situation apply, and what are the time deadlines for action in your area?

15. Mr. White calls about his son, Steven, who was sent home early from school because of behavior problems and wonders if you can push the Child Guidance Clinic to prescribe tranquilizers for him. How do you follow up?

16. A white mother of a fourteen-year-old trainable mentally retarded girl is highly concerned. She says her daughter has a black boyfriend in the neighboring school district, in which her daughter attends special education classes. She wants her daughter immediately placed in a residential girls' school. How do you respond to her?

17. A mother of a regular junior high student contacts you, after you have made a most stimulating speech at a PTA meeting, and tells you she is worried that her daughter is "headed for trouble." She would like to discuss her concern, but she has small children at home and no car. She asks if someone can make a home call? How do you respond?

18. Mr. Bryant, a young male school social worker, asks to meet with you "today." He comes, clearly agitated, and says the father of a student who is on his caseload has threatened to name him in his divorce suit as the third party, and that he has alienated his wife's affections. Mr. Bryant says there is no foundation to the charge, that he has simply made house calls and talked to the mother about her child. He says the mother does call him frequently. What actions do you take?

19. A one week special education summer camp at a state park one hundred miles away is planned. A parental meeting is scheduled to give information. What should be the agenda for the meeting?

20. Some parents want to sit in on the individual curriculum planning meeting for their child. Do you allow this, and if so, what role should they play at the meeting?

21. A new special education teacher candidate asks if you expect teachers to make home visits. Do you? Why?

SUGGESTED GUIDELINES FOR ACTIONS

1. A pet, such as a dog, can become a good object for a child to show his affection, if he needs some emotional help in this area.

2. If special service personnel home visits regarding children are seriously thought to be "romantic" visits, immediately change the worker in the situation and assign someone of a different sex. Have the special service worker in question halt all contacts to that home.

3. Follow up personal meetings with parents with a letter outlining point by point the agreements reached. Indicate if there are any misunderstandings regarding the agreements listed. The parent should check with you within forty-eight hours of receiving the letter.

4. Parents can and should be involved in developing individual pupil plans with the professional team. They should be considered equal, well-respected team members.

5. Teachers should be encouraged to visit the homes of their students.

6. Encourage the most positive staff attitudes toward parents.

7. Pupil evaluations should be immediately followed by sharing information with the parents.

8. Give parents some specific information about what action you plan to take and when they can expect additional response if called for by the situation.

9. Have all pupil schedule changes go through an educational planning committee.

10. Teachers should not be free to switch pupils to less than a full day regular schedule without appropriate consultation.

11. Save a lot of phone calls by getting all details regarding the fall schedule (teacher, building assignment, daily hours, bus schedule, etc) in a preschool letter.

12. Develop positive plans of action with the parents and provide for a future follow up evaluation meeting.

13. Share happy news with parents as often as possible in your school system.

14. Know the legal system, and the officials involved, in your area.

Chapter 7

RELATIONSHIPS WITH GENERAL EDUCATION

THE REQUESTS FOR ACTION

1. Miss Long, the principal of Webster School, with six elementary classes for the educable mentally retarded, asks you what her responsibility is to these rooms. She wonders if you will be taking care of them. How should you respond?

2. The special education teachers in Miss Long's building ask if they should attend her staff meetings. They say they are bored with a lot of content which is not relevant to them. Should they? Why?

3. You need to develop a special education handbook with information which the various building administrators and regular teachers should know, regarding special education and services. What do you think should be the table of contents?

4. You decide to have a committee develop the general contents of the special education handbook. What roles or persons would you place on the committee?

5. The mother of a twelve-year-old girl in regular education tells you she has just found out her daughter steals. The mother found a teacher's billfold in her trash can. She took it to the

teacher who suggested she call you. She wants advice on how to handle her daughter. How do you respond?

6. A regular junior high teacher asks if she can borrow a Language Master machine from a special education classroom for the weekend to use in one of her university classes. What is your policy?

7. The community school agent tells you that an elementary teacher has a refrigerator to donate to a special education class. Where do you decide to send it? Why?

8. A high school student wants to do an independent project on special education. What else should you find out from her. What potential projects might be most appropriate for her?

9. A parochial school principal in Hazelwood needs individual materials to give Frostig tests, which are requested before referral for psychological testing. Do you provide materials to parochial schools?

10. The cerebral palsy day school informs you that a five year old from Hazelwood, who is attending their program, should be tried in regular kindergarten next fall. What procedures do you follow to arrange for this? Do you provide any supportive services?

11. Superintendent Goodenough asks if you wish to be fully responsible for interviewing and recommending special education and special service teacher candidates for employment; or do you wish to have them processed the same way general education teacher candidates are processed for potential employment?

12. The special education teachers are paid an additional two hundred dollars beyond the regular salary scale for their level of experience and training. How do you justify this when asked by the principals at an administrative council meeting?

13. Mr. Hilley, the Hoover principal, wants to move a special education classroom into a smaller room so that he can give the larger space to a regular class. Do you agree to this?

14. The regular sixth graders in the building where the elementary educable mentally retarded are placed are going camping. The teacher of the similar aged special education group asks what you think about requesting that her group accompany them to camp. What do you think?

15. The teacher of the orthopedically handicapped asks for suggestions to begin integrating her pupils with regular classes. What suggestions do you have?

16. Last year you had a very ineffective special education teacher in a building with just the one elementary special education classroom. The regular staff and students have a low image of special education. You have a new teacher in that room in the fall with whom you discuss the situation, since she tells you her students have been ridiculed on the playground. What activities could she organize to build up the image of the special education students in that building?

17. The elementary teachers in one building take turns with playground supervision, including the special education teachers whose children play on the playground at the same time. A special education teacher is concerned since one regular teacher confronts her if she has even a simple discipline problem with a

special education student. The teacher says she does not know how to handle the special education students. What should the special education teacher do?

18. The assistant principal at the high school asks you to sit in on an afternoon of individual sessions, each six weeks period, with high school students who have been having problems (such as excessive absenteeism). The principal wants you to suggest which ones might be referred for some special services. Do you do this, and if so, what information do you request?

19. A principal asks you if it is permissible to provide reverse integration in his building, i.e. to send regular students with reading problems into the special education classroom for special reading instruction. Do you allow this?

20. The Director of Instruction for the school district is going to appoint some curriculum committees to develop a curriculum guide on subject areas. He asks if he should appoint any special education teachers to the committees. Should he?

SUGGESTED GUIDELINES FOR ACTIONS

1. Principals should have the same responsibilities toward special education classroom programs in their buildings as they do toward the regular classrooms in their buildings.

2. Special education teachers should attend the building staff meetings along with regular classroom teachers. Arrangements may be made for special interest subgroups during parts of staff meeting time.

3. Keep committees small.

4. Be sure committees include persons who can empathize with the needs of the audience toward whom their efforts are directed.

5. Remember to delegate responsibility to the appropriate persons and then refer requests to them.

6. A personal visit by the family and child to a program in which a child may be enrolled is helpful.

7. Involve the building principal in all planning and implementation phases for integration of special education students with regular students.

8. Integration should be with similar aged pupils.

9. Plan integration on an individual basis.

10. Integrate where you feel the special education student stands a good chance of being successful.

11. Provide basic information to the regular teachers regarding the nature of the special education students in their building.

12. Be familiar with all state regulations regarding special education, especially those dealing with eligible students and teacher assignments.

13. Always check in at the principal's office when you enter a school building.

14. Keep the principals well informed of special education and special service activities.

15. Encourage high school students to enter the special education profession.

16. Take an active part, if possible, in the employment of personnel for the program you direct.

17. Make sure building principals are involved in the selection process of special education teachers for their building.

18. Be able to justify realistically any preferential differences between special education and regular education.

19. Don't tolerate a "second class citizen" approach to services for the handicapped. Take definite steps to build positive images of the handicapped.

Chapter 8

BOARD OF EDUCATION

THE REQUESTS FOR ACTION

1. Superintendent Goodenough has asked you to take fifteen minutes of the school board agenda time to describe the special education and special service program to the board. Who would you involve in making the presentation? What visual materials would you use?

2. The Superintendent asks if you have any items for the next school board agenda. Suggest a specific item that would be appropriate.

3. Mr. Biddle, the Garden School principal, and you are to recommend that the board provide a regular diploma (rather than a special certificate) to graduates of the special education program. A background report for the board supporting this recommendation is needed. What would be the outline of such a report?

4. A school board member asks to visit some of the special education programs for a couple of hours one morning. Arrange such a visit schedule for the maximum benefit of the board member.

5. The Garden School staff has asked for a greenhouse class-

room program, with a greenhouse to be added to the existing school structure. How would you justify the value of this program to the school board?

6. The board wants to know the estimated cost of the proposed greenhouse classroom, since it is not the usual type of construction, and if the staff knows what companies would do the construction. What information can you give them?

7. You are asking the school board to establish a new role of an elementary special education curriculum supervisor. What reasons do you give for needing such a person?

8. It is school board election time and two candidates are vying for one position. You definitely prefer one of them who is a backer of special education programs. What efforts could you make in that candidate's behalf?

9. The state is clamping down on dull normal level pupils being enrolled in classes for the educable mentally retarded. You have five or six such pupils enrolled in classes for the educable mentally retarded, for whom you must make other provisions in the school system. A board member requests a report on this situation with recommended remedial actions. What remedial actions could you suggest?

10. You are being interviewed by the board of education for the position of director of special education. The board asks you, if you are selected for this position in Hazelwood, what efforts would you make to coordinate special education with general education. What is your response?

11. At a board meeting, one of the board members asks you

what is the policy regarding school exclusions. Indicate to him what the state law indicates regarding exclusions. He also asks if you recommend a policy which expands on the state law. Respond.

12. You want more opportunities for contact between the board of education members and the special education staff members. How can you arrange for this?

13. A parent whose child has been formally excluded from school asks to meet with the board of education to appeal the decision. What arrangements would you make for this encounter?

14. The county or intermediate school district group of directors of special education is planning a special education informational meeting for the intermediate school district board of education. You are one of three directors who will be handling the session. What topics would you cover at this two-hour session and how would they be divided among the three directors, you, Mr. Stringer and Mrs. Blake?

15. A board of education member asks about a neighbor's child who was found not eligible for the special education class for the emotionally disturbed. The board member thinks the child is disturbed and asks you to have the educational planning committee reconsider the case. He says the child is driving his parents crazy with his misbehavior and is always getting into trouble. Do you agree to do this? Are there other services which might be provided?

16. The upper elementary class for the educable mentally retarded has learned to make beautiful walnut bowls. The teacher suggests making one for each board member for a Christmas present. Is this a good idea?

17. Before each board meeting, the board meets with the superintendent for thirty minutes for a presession briefing. Do you feel you should ask to be involved in this briefing?

18. The State Board of Education is considering its position regarding the proposed new law mandating special education. You have been invited to present some pro and con factors to the state board regarding this proposed legislation. Suggest two or three issues you might raise on both sides.

19. During the "Other" section of the school board agenda, a new board member asks about a particular pupil who has been having great school difficulties. A reporter and some community members are in the audience. How do you handle this?

20. Accountability is being discussed at the board meeting. A board member asks you how you assure accountability with special education and special services programs. How do you?

SUGGESTED GUIDELINES FOR ACTIONS

1. Deal honestly with all people, including the board of education.

2. Keep the board of education informed about special education and special service programs.

3. Involve your staff members in presentations to the board of education.

4. Know the rules for board of education functioning, including the time schedule for presentation of new policy items. Some rules must be presented in two consecutive meetings.

5. In writing reports, keep the reader in mind.

6. Whenever possible, give the board members background reading materials before issues are discussed.

7. If you do not know the answer to a question, wait until you get the facts to respond. Don't try to respond in ignorance.

8. Support the policies of the Board of Education, or work quietly with the board to get needed policy changes, with the approval of the superintendent.

9. Keep the superintendent informed of your contacts with school board members.

10. Always serve as an advocate of the handicapped.

11. Keep public presentations interesting, using visual demonstrations wherever possible. Keep in mind key points of information to be shared.

12. Do not divulge confidential information about the individual pupils at public meetings.

Chapter 9

RELATIONSHIPS WITH OTHER AGENCIES

THE REQUESTS FOR ACTION

1. The state institution for the mentally retarded, which serves your area, has a new policy advocating the concept of short-term residential placement. They have suggested the need to develop a communication system with the school district for school aged residents at the institution in order to facilitate the patient's return to the community. What method could you suggest?

2. You are considering sharing the services of one of your school social workers with the neighboring school district in order to get the state required school membership coverage necessary for this professional role. How would you suggest the time and responsibilities be divided? What details would need to be clarified between districts?

3. The public health nurses have been asked to serve as the liaison for your school for referrals to physicians for neurological examinations. These examinations are required as part of the pupil certification process for entrance into the Perceptual Development Program for the neurologically impaired. The nurse tells you one family doesn't have the money for such an examination. To what resources could you refer her for the money?

4. The director of special education of the neighboring school

district which serves some of your pupils, tells you that they need new orders on Barbara Ball from the United Cerebral Palsy Clinic. How do you arrange to get the new orders for therapy?

5. The director of services for the blind at the state library is sending you some materials for the blind, and she requests you to send her a list of the students served. Is there any reason why you can not release these names to her?

6. The community mental health director invites you to be a member of a professional advisory group for "Day Care for the Emotionally Disturbed." Do you accept?

7. The county association for retarded citizens invites you to serve as a member of its education committee. Should you? Why?

8. A special education professor at a state university, which is a ninety minute drive from Hazelwood, asks if he can bring forty seniors in mental retardation to visit both elementary and secondary programs for the retarded in your school district. They would come by bus and spend one day in Hazelwood. They want program tours, lunch provisions and follow up discussion time. Arrange their schedule.

9. The division of vocational rehabilitation liaison person from the intermediate school district office wants to do a narcotics survey at the two junior high school buildings, the senior high and Garden School. What arangements need to be made for this if your school system agrees to allow it to be done?

10. A physician requests, for his information, an audiometer

test on a five-year-old patient from Hazelwood. Do you supply this for him through your speech correctionist?

11. A mother from a neighboring school district asks if you can accept her fifteen-year-old daughter in your secondary special education program as a nonresident. She says the girl was on Doman Delacato method and can not tolerate a full day of school. How would you respond?

12. The community mental health board asks you to provide in-service education for their staff of ten, in the program for the severely retarded, for one evening each week. They propose to contract with you to do this. You want to explore their needs before making a decision. How do you do this?

13. Mr. Biddle, the Garden School principal, wants the division of vocational rehabilitation to pay for in-school employment training programs for the mentally retarded, such as laundry service training. Explore this possibility in your state.

14. The State Association for Children with Learning Disabilities wants to start a chapter in Hazelwood. How do you suggest they proceed to explore this?

15. The county community college has proposed a two-year preparation program for aides to work with the mentally retarded. Their planning document lists you as a participant in developing the plan. You only attended one meeting, and then the community college staff developed and published the plan without further consultation with the outside group (which met once). You are angry at being listed as a developer of the plan, since you do not consider it to be well done. What constructive action could you take?

16. A state department of education consultant informs you that a fifteen-year-old boy in Garden School called him long distance and told him you were forcing him to take swimming and the boy thinks he will drown. He said some boys pushed him in the pool, bruised him and he had seen a doctor regarding the bruise. The state consultant asks that you check this out and call him back. How do you proceed?

17. A state special education consultant asks if you can send an upper elementary teacher of the educable mentally retarded to a meeting next week to help plan a conference. Do you agree to do this, and if so, what arrangements need to be made?

18. A member of the "Community Relations Committee" of the community mental health board invites you to meet with the committee to suggest additional needed services which might be sponsored by community mental health. What services might you suggest?

19. The vision consultant from the state department of public health wants to discuss a possible demonstration program in your district regarding dyslexia with slow learners. What areas or issues might you discuss with him?

20. The community worker from the state institution for the mentally retarded tells you that the family of a high school special education student needs counseling regarding the student. What other details do you need to find out?

21. Six parents from outside of your school district, who are members of the county association for retarded citizens, ask to visit your program for the retarded. Do you let them, and if so, what arrangements do you make?

22. A private school for the emotionally disturbed, which is located in a neighboring school district, requests your school district to sponsor their program, and thereby receive state aid from the department of education. How do you respond? Why?

23. A university student, who also does substitute teaching in Hazelwood, wants information for a term paper on "Nursery Schools." How do you help her out?

24. The psychologist, who teaches driver education to the special education students during the summer, says he is having problems with the office of the secretary of state regarding the pupils' examinations for a license. The state has an agreement that illiterate persons may receive an oral examination. However, this particular office requires that the test first be administered in writing at the school. If the student fails the written test, he must go to Traffic School one night and then take another written test. If the student again fails, he may then take an oral test of fifty true or false questions. The instructor wants the oral test for those who need it immediately when he recommends it, rather than have the two frustrating hurdles when the instructor already knows which ones can not read. What steps do you take to correct this situation?

25. An older wheelchair bound student in your orthopedic program wants arrangements made for her to take a typing class this summer in the neighboring school district. What arrangements need to be made?

26. The Youth Protection Agency in your community wants to start a "Big Brother or Sister" type of program for school aged troubled youths, who may be headed for the courts, and asks your advice and help in establishing this type of program. Make some suggestions for getting this program started.

27. One of the probate court judges approaches you about the feasibility of starting a "half-way-type house" in your area for adolescent boys who have been in trouble and referred to the court, and whose problems seem to stem from an unsupervised home situation. He asks for suggestions about numbers of boys to be served, room requirements, staff requirements and a proposed daily schedule, including planning for weekends. He wants to involve the total community as much as possible. What suggestions do you have for him?

SUGGESTED GUIDELINES FOR ACTIONS

1. A regular system of communication should be established with any other agency providing services to school aged residents of your district, including a residential placement outside of your immediate area.

2. Shared programs with other school districts should have a key administrator with responsibility for the program.

3. All potential financial resources, which may help to better serve the pupils, should be explored.

4. Know the laws regarding confidentiality and provisions for release of information in your state.

5. Share your skills wherever possible with other community agencies, such as by serving on their committees. Ask for reciprocity where appropriate.

6. Clear visits to special education programs with the building principals. The principals should clear these visits with the teachers involved.

7. Plan ahead as much as possible for formal meetings and include time for group movement, personal needs, etc.

8. Make sure requested changes in school schedules, or requested time outside of school schedules, have legitimate purposes.

9. Cooperate wherever possible with persons attempting to evaluate your pupils.

10. Referrals for nonresident placements in your system should always go through the special education administrator of the other school system.

11. Make sure that in-service education for any group is directed towards its specific needs.

12. If you are concerned about someone's inappropriate actions, first discuss that concern with that person.

13. Keep your sense of humor.

14. Delegate responsibilities and have faith that people will perform well.

15. Know the legally potential services of other agencies, so you can make appropriate requests for additional services.

16. Share your programs with others and show pride in what the team has developed.

17. Utilize family resources in helping to plan for services wherever possible.

COMMUNITY RESOURCES, COMMITTEES AND PUBLIC RELATIONS

THE REQUESTS FOR ACTION

1. A state legislator from your area wants to visit the special education program and learn some of the financial facts about special education. What is the state aid formula for each classroom in your program?

2. The Governor is to visit your school district to learn about volunteer programs sponsored by the school. What roles do, or could, volunteers perform in your special education program?

3. The Community School Director, Mr. Keane, asks if you have a special education advisory council, and if so, who is on it. How do you respond?

4. You are starting a Title Six program for the preschool multiply handicapped and need to find eligible pupils. Prepare a news release requesting community referrals of eligible pupils.

5. The area newspaper invites you to provide a series for them of ten articles on special education. How would you do it? Indicate topics to cover in each and provide the first article.

6. One of your teachers wants a large carpet for a reading corner in her room. Funds are short, so what approaches could you use to obtain this for her?

7. On Wednesday, the community school agent informs you that the Kiwanis Club has donated 150 circus tickets which include admission, beverage, hot dog and popcorn. The circus is next Monday and is ten miles away. What arrangements do you make and with whom?

8. The Hazelwood city recreation department says the AMVETS have donated 100 tickets to "Fireman's Field Day" on Saturday at the stadium ten miles away. They will bus anyone going. How do you use these tickets and what arrangements do you need to make?

9. A university student from your area would like to observe an educational planning meeting for a special education student. Do you allow this? What factors do you take into consideration in making your decision?

10. A lady from your area inquires if you can use her old Christmas cards. What do you tell her?

11. Mrs. Mitchell, the mother of a special education student, has clothing she would like to donate to someone in need. What do you tell her to do with it?

12. Mrs. Spector, a lady from the community calls and says she wants to tell someone (she is starting with you) about the deplorably filthy condition in the home of her neighbor. To whom do you refer her?

13. The high school principal, Mr. Proud, is concerned about a twenty-eight-year-old male who had been "kicked out of school at fifteen years and does nothing." His needs are great, including the need for dentures, as he is toothless. Can you connect him with the proper resources?

14. Your elementary level teachers of the mentally retarded are concerned that not enough special education parents are involved in the PTA, and that the PTA meetings are not well planned. What can you suggest they do to help correct both problems?

15. A junior high school teacher of the emotionally disturbed wants to start a "foster grandparent" program for his students who come from unstable home environments. He asks about contacting the city recreation department person in charge of their senior citizen program. What do you think of this project, and what suggestions do you have to make it effective?

16. A lady in the community asks about your possible need for her volunteer services to teach dancing and rhythm to the handicapped. You decide to start with one trial group. What group do you select and why?

17. A television station wants to do a segment on special education and the handicapped, and asks if they can take pictures of two or three of your special education classes in action, plus interview a school social worker. Do you allow this, and if so, what precautions do you employ?

18. There is a community beautification project, with a citizen as volunteer chairman of a community committee. You are asked to serve on the committee and to suggest projects for the schools.

What projects might you suggest? How would special education be involved?

19. The nearby privately operated sheltered workshop serves several mentally retarded individuals from your area. They invite you to serve on their board of directors. Do you? What information do you need in making your decision?

20. Your staff wants to have a special education open house for the community. How do you help organize this?

SUGGESTED GUIDELINES FOR ACTIONS

1. Know the financial facts behind the special education program.
2. Promote your program with pride.
3. Encourage visitors to your program.
4. Make maximum use of volunteer community resources, if they can make a positive contribution to the program.
5. Keep the community informed about special education and special service programs.
6. Use news releases wisely and write them with the readers in mind.
7. For a series of articles, utilize staff talents and develop a general format to follow in each article.
8. Ask for appropriate donations, particularly from the businesses in your area.
9. Take advantage of gifts from service clubs.
10. Suggest needed projects to service clubs which will help the handicapped.
11. Have confidence in team work and being able to meet deadlines.
12. In so far as possible, plan ahead for specific details in each activity.
13. Know the laws regarding confidentiality of individual information.

14. Know appropriate community resources for referrals of questions which are not appropriate for your office to handle.

15. Encourage your staff to assume leadership roles in the community.

16. Solicit the help of all organized groups in your area, and ask them what type of projects they may be seeking.

Chapter 11

TRANSPORTATION

THE REQUESTS FOR ACTION

1. The bus supervisor has requested a list of special education students who ride the bus, who are allergic to wasp or bee stings. Specify how you would obtain this information.

2. It is five P.M. Thursday, and the bus supervisor tells you that the parents were not notified that the Friday afternoon session of the preschool class will not meet. What do you do about notifying the families?

3. The bus supervisor informs you that an obese mentally retarded pupil has a terribly offensive feces-like odor on the bus, and asks if you can do something about the situation. How would you handle this?

4. A large old bus is being used to transport a small group of special education students to other districts. The bus supervisor wants the school district to arrange to buy a new, or relatively new, small bus. How do you proceed with this in your school system?

5. The director of special education from the neighboring school district, which serves some of your pupils, is concerned

because a seven-year-old deaf, mentally retarded, and neurologically impaired pupil from Hazelwood is arriving on the bus too early and spends a long unsupervised time on the playground. He is afraid the boy might have a seizure. How can you resolve this?

6. The bus supervisor tells you in alarm that a boy had a seizure on the bus. What action is called for on your part and what additional information do you need?

7. You learn that a deaf Hazelwood student is a persistent behavioral problem on the bus. The student is transported by a private bus service with whom you contract. What action would be appropriate for you to take?

8. You learn that the private bus system is carrying fourteen passengers in a nine seat capacity vehicle. What steps do you take to correct this?

9. The bus supervisor tell you that two special education boys were in a fight on the bus. One was hit on the head and has a lump. What should be done?

10. A neighboring school district to which you send, by bus, special education pupils, calls to tell you they won't have school on Friday. They have notified the pupils. What else needs to be done?

11. Two students reported that the bus driver "swore and told the kids they were all nuts, and that is why they are coming here to school." What do you do about this?

12. A neighboring school district wants to have your special

education students, who attend their program during the regular year, also attend summer school. What problems might you have in arranging transportation? Also, why might you want them to attend your own summer school instead?

13. The bus supervisor asks you to make a fifteen minute presentation at the intermediate school system's orientation training session for new bus drivers in the county on "What the Special Education Pupil is Like." Outline your presentation.

14. You have a summer program planning committee. Should the bus supervisor be a regular member of the committee or invited to one or two meetings only? What factors could his decisions affect in your summer program?

15. Some of the bus pupils are riding, for what seems to you, an unnecessarily long time. You decide to investigate. What methods would you use to investigate?

16. A new bus driver seems to be having many problems with the special education students, according to the special education teachers. What specific actions would be appropriate to help resolve this?

17. A bus driver is having difficulty manipulating a wheelchair student off the bus. The family gets him on the bus. What suggestions could you make to ease this situation?

18. A student from the class for the emotionally disturbed keeps swearing at the bus driver. It is making the bus driver quite angry. What actions might be taken regarding this and by whom?

19. The older trainable mentally retarded could ride the public bus to the sheltered workshop. What skills should be taught them to have them effectively use this means of transportation?

20. At a meeting of parents of the older trainable mentally retarded, you are asked if they might have driver education training. How do you respond and what reasons do you give?

SUGGESTED GUIDELINES FOR ACTIONS

1. Requests for information should be clear, with a deadline indicated for the response.

2. Delegate to the responsible staff member.

3. Use the services of public health nurses for health problems.

4. Know the school system procedure for requesting needed items, including which items need the approval of the school board.

5. Be gutsy about exploring nonschool resources.

6. Cooperate with other school personnel and communicate informally with them whenever possible.

7. Provide orientation information to bus drivers regarding the handling of special education pupils.

8. Provide accurate information to all professional and non-professional staff regarding what to do in case of seizures.

9. Involve parents in all phases of the program, including helping to correct behavioral problems.

10. Always insist on safe transportation provisions for special education pupils.

11 Make sure your transportation provisions are in accordance with the state laws.

12. Immediately notify the parents when medical attention may be required.

13. When you receive a complaint, check with the other party(ies) concerned.

14. Utilize people only when they are needed on a committee.

15. Involve others in researching all possible suggestions for solutions to problems.

16. Don't overlook the simplest details in teaching special education pupils how to use public transportation. For instance, in addition to showing them how to get somewhere, also show them how to return. Insist on concrete teaching methods.

17. Be honest with all those with whom you deal, especially parents.

Chapter 12

HOUSING

THE REQUESTS FOR ACTION

1. Mr. Wood, the Roosevelt School principal, tells you he needs the room that the trainable mentally retarded are in for next year, due to enrollment increases in his area. Make plans to move the one class. How would you select the new building for this program?

2. One choice, of several, is to place the trainable program in a portable classroom. What are the pros and cons of placing it there?

3. You need a room to start an elementary program for the neurologically handicapped (or Perceptual Development Program). What would you tell the principals you are looking for in room size, basic equipment and other important areas of information?

4. You are planning an addition to an elementary building which will include two special education rooms for the trainable mentally retarded. What features would you want in these rooms?

5. The school social worker coordinator indicates there is an

urgent need for a space, other than the social workers' office, for the consulting psychiatrist to conduct his interviews and to meet with the special service staff. She suggests a section of the hall near their office be partitioned for this. What do you think?

6. Mr. Dombrose, the teacher in charge of the new greenhouse, is angry. He says there is no water, nor electricity; the sink is still in the carton and there is no heat. He says everything is marked by lengthy delays. Who should be contacted regarding this?

7. Matty Miller, of "Project Scope," a nonprofit organization sponsoring a group discussion project for troubled teens, asks for space once a week for two hours in any of your elementary schools for the group meetings. Do you comply?

8. The vision consultant from the state department of public health brings a light meter during a visit to your school district and shows you how dim (below the recommended number of candlelights) your special education classrooms are with all of the lights turned on. What do you do about this?

9. There will be a new position at the high school; a teacher counselor for the emotionally disturbed. The professional will work with individuals or with small groups. What type of housing provision should be requested?

10. A room is available in an elementary school to initiate the preschool classroom for the multiply handicapped. However, the toilet facility is down the hall. You have an option of moving a teacher with many years seniority out of her classroom (midyear) to obtain her room with the toilet facility. What factors do you take into consideration in making the decision. Who else would be involved in the decision-making process?

11. A new two story addition is planned at one of the two junior high school buildings, including a library and other classrooms. State law requires an elevator, for access to the physically handicapped, which would cost at least ten thousand dollars extra. The elevator requirement would be waived if you indicate that all physically handicapped would be served at the other one story junior high school which is across town. Do you agree to this? Why?

12. Your special service staff is enlarging and you have two or more per office. You have an option of providing more adequate office space by scattering the special service personnel to various buildings. What factors do you consider in making this decision?

13. The intermediate school district has purchased a former bowling alley which will be renovated into a school building for the older trainable mentally retarded pupils. You are asked to suggest types and sizes of room provisions they will need. What suggestions do you have?

14. The State Department of Education is revising its rules and regulations for special education. You are working on a leadership committee for this purpose. A question has come up regarding what regulations to have regarding housing for the educable mentally retarded. What recommendations do you make?

15. A neighboring school district is including plans for an orthopedic suite to serve three groups in a new elementary building. A delegation from their district visits your facility and discusses their plans. What things do you tell them they should be sure to include in their building plans in order to provide quality services?

16. You have a choice of two classrooms for the new program for the neurologically handicapped. You will serve ten to twelve-year-old upper elementary pupils at first. One classroom choice is a large room with toilet and sink provisions in the wing of the building with younger pupils. The other choice is a small upstairs room without toilet facilities, but located near similar aged pupils. Which room do you choose? Why?

17. All six of your elementary classes for the educable mentally retarded are in one elementary building. What are the advantages and disadvantages of this?

18. A new suite of rooms for the deaf and hard of hearing is being planned in another school system in your county which will serve all such handicapped persons in the county. What provisions are a must to be included in the construction plans?

19. The teacher of the elementary level emotionally disturbed pupils has a large classroom with toilet facilities. He asks to move to a smaller classroom without a toilet which is available in the same building, saying it will be easier to control his group with less space. Do you agree to this? Why?

20. Garden School has a suite of three rooms (one large and two small) which are to be developed into a unit to teach health and family care and nurse aide skills. What equipment features do you want included in these three rooms?

SUGGESTED GUIDELINES FOR ACTIONS

1. If feasible, locate classes near the homes of the majority of the class enrollment.

2. Special education classrooms should be of comparable size to regular classrooms to provide space for the variety of activities that occur in such programs.

3. Involve teachers and special education supervisors in planning new classroom facilities.

4. Have a good general knowledge of all physical facilities in your school system so you can readily pinpoint resources.

5. Know who is the responsible administrator to approve the use of facilities for nonschool groups. Obtain a sample copy of the request form if there is one.

6. Special services rooms may be small, but should have privacy and be free of extemporaneous noise distractions.

7. Attempt to obtain the good will of the total building staff toward a new special education program in that facility.

8. Do not displace a regular classroom in the middle of the year for a new special education class.

9. If possible, provide your special service staff with office space where they can informally communicate with each other, and with other disciplines periodically.

10. Special education student housing provisions should differ from the normal only when necessary for their best interests. For instance, special education students should be housed near regular classes with similar chronological aged pupils.

11. Consider remodeling potential, such as adding a sink, when looking at possible special education classrooms.

12. Housing facilities should enhance the instructional program.

Chapter 13

FINANCES

THE REQUESTS FOR ACTION

1. Miss Long, the Webster School principal, is concerned about special education children receiving milk, if needed, and having warm clothes. She asks if you can help arrange for these needs, especially the milk, if it is not ordered. How would you do this?

2. You are initiating a new classroom for the neurologically handicapped. How much money do you request for an initial order of equipment and supplies?

3. There is a school millage issue. The superintendent suggests you contact special education parents and request their support. Suggest several possible methods for dealing with this.

4. You are requesting a federal grant for a preschool program for the multiply handicapped. Specify your requested budget items.

5. A mentally retarded, emotionally disturbed boy needs residential placement. The family is short 100 dollars per month, of the total charge of 160 dollars per month, of making the payments. Where could you seek this additional needed amount?

6. A teacher of elementary mentally retarded pupils asks for a voucher to purchase groceries for the summer camping program. How would you arrange for this and how much would you request for one week of camp for 100 students plus staff?

7. The school social worker coordinator says the consulting psychiatrist hasn't received his monthly check. The approval is processed at the school board meeting. How would you check this out and respond?

8. The school business manager asks you to justify to him the fact that special education teacher aides are paid fifty cents more per hour than regular classroom teacher aides. Can you do so?

9. A speech correctionist is worried since she hasn't received reimbursement for the conference she attended. What would be the process for submission, approval and reimbursement of such expenses?

10. A lunchroom aide for the elementary educable mentally retarded program has a second group of fifteen extra pupils to supervise during today's lunch hour. She feels she should receive extra pay. How do you react?

11. An elementary level teacher of the educable mentally retarded is out of work, still ill from a back injury she received at work last year. She has filed for workmen's compensation. She says she is not getting the difference between her pay and a substitute teacher's pay as she understands she should. How would you check this out?

12. Several teachers have received state grants which are

administered by the school district to enable them to take special education classes at the university. The grants are paid before class enrollment. One teacher tells you she did not enroll for a class after she received her grant due to some unexpected circumstances. She wonders what is the proper procedure to follow in repaying the money. Tell her.

13. The teacher/counselor for the physically handicapped needs an electric typewriter for a physically handicapped student at the junior high school. How would this be arranged?

14. The elementary supervisor, Mr. Foote, tells you that the orthopedic room's wheelchairs, which are the property of the school district, have been used for five years and need inspection and repair. He has a list of chair numbers and replacement parts needed. What procedure should be used to effect this needed service?

15. The payroll office asks you what pay schedule you are using for your summer special education staff. Is it an hourly rate, or their regular salary prorated? Which is it?

16. You want to include in a presentation the actual per pupil cost for a specific special education classroom program. What direct and indirect cost items would be included in the computation?

17. Some visiting university special education students ask you to tell them the system of state reimbursement for your special education programs. Do so, and also include information about potential sources of funds.

18. You understand there are potential state funds for special

projects under vocational education. Obtain this information from the State Department of Education, including total funds currently available, application deadlines, reimbursement formula and scope of acceptable projects.

19. You want to initiate the position of elementary special education supervisor for curriculum leadership. What type of reimbursement can you get from both state and intermediate school district sources?

20. You are a member of the legislative committee of the state association of administrators of special education. What committees in your state legislature are particularly important for you to work with in terms of special education legislation?

21. You have a petty cash sum for miscellaneous small purchases. What suggestions would you have for the use of this fund.

SUGGESTED GUIDELINES FOR ACTIONS

1. Know the details in the regular system for obtaining items for the needy.
2. Actively involve citizens in working toward the successful passage of needed school millage issues.
3. Follow the format in the agency information packet when developing budget requests for grants.
4. Know public and private financial resources at all levels which may supplement school monies to provide more services for the pupils.
5. Have a justified rationale for variations in financial reimbursement patterns for special education staff.
6. Make sure your staff is familiar with the procedure and time schedule for claiming reimbursements.
7. If you don't know an answer, say so without hesitation,

and check it out directly with the persons responsible for having the information.

8. Make use of vouchers from the business office to quickly obtain needed items or services.

9. Check periodically with surrounding school districts to see how they handle financial details, such as petty cash, summer wages, teacher differentials, etc.

10. Know the financial details of the special education program.

11. Obtain receipts for reimbursed items, including items purchased with the petty cash fund.

12. Be twice as conscientious and accountable with your business finances as you are with your personal finances.

FORMS AND RECORDS

THE REQUESTS FOR ACTION

1. The special service referral forms need to be revised. How would you proceed?

2. Superintendent Goodenough asks you to confer with his secretary, who handles teacher certification matters for the school system, regarding the procedures to follow for approval of the special education staff. The teachers must meet regular certification standards plus state special education approval. What do you tell the secretary is the proper process to use to make sure all your staff meets state standards?

3. An elementary school secretary asks about integrated students who are enrolled in both special education and regular classes for part of each day. She wants to know which teacher should keep the attendance records.

4. The special education report cards appear ineffective in their current format. How would you go about revising them? How would you relate this project to general education?

5. A parent of a child who is to enter your preschool program asks if the child needs a physical. Does he?

6. A mother of a special education student informs you she is moving. She wants to take information regarding her son's special education placement to the new school system. What do you give her?

7. Mr. Foote, the elementary special education supervisor, tells you that an elementary level teacher of the educable mentally retarded was bowling with her class, and fell down, injuring herself. X-rays were taken. He asks if there is school insurance for this and if she should complete an accident report. What information can you give him?

8. A police detective from the next town stops in to see if you can give him information regarding a former Hazelwood student. He wants to know if the man was enrolled in special education and what his problems were. Do you give him any information?

9. The intermediate school district requests that you send all test protocols to them of a boy your office has referred for a psychiatric evaluation. Do you send this information to them?

10. One of the speech correctionists wants to know if you want a regular monthly caseload report. Do you? Why?

11. A high school counselor tells you that copies of psychological reports have been sent to juvenile court with a signed release by the high school. Do you want to follow that procedure, or do you want all special service records sent out through your offices?

12. One of the psychologists is concerned about psychological reports which are sent to other school districts. She says she

would like to rewrite all reports sent out of the district. Her reasons are hazy. How do you respond?

13. The teacher/counselor for the physically handicapped wants to know where to make notations on the individual pupil cumulative folder since there is no category for her special service. Check your state cumulative folder forms and suggest where she might write her comments.

14. In the spring, an elementary principal wants to know what, if anything, you want on the report cards of the pupils in regular grades who will be enrolled in special education classes in the fall. What do you want on them?

15. A question is raised as to who should handle nontenure special education classroom teacher evaluations and also non-tenure special services personnel evaluations. Who should be responsible for this?

16. The intermediate school district director of special education wants your special education prospectus for next year by January nineteenth. What process do you use in developing such a plan for special education programs and services for next year?

17. A special services consultant from the State Department of Education tells you that your application forms indicate you do not have the necessary membership backing of twenty-five hundred pupils for each of your four school social workers. You are about five hundred pupils short. You indicate you will formally apply for an exception from this rule due to extenuating circumstances in your school district. Indicate the reasons you need more than the state allotment of school social workers.

18. You decide it will be helpful to you to have a listing, by date due, of all special education forms required by the state and county. Make such a list.

19. You need a form for the files to indicate the decisions made by educational placement and planning committees. What should be on this form?

20. You decide to make a form letter with instructions for all new teacher applicants, which will be originally typed each time. Develop such a form letter, with instructions for the applicant.

SUGGESTED GUIDELINES FOR ACTIONS

1. Small committees usually are effective in developing forms.

2. Involve regular education staff in the development of forms they will be using.

3. Parents should be involved with professionals in determining the content of report cards.

4. Know the school system's provisions for staff injuries.

5. Do not give out confidential information regarding pupils without signed release forms or a court order.

6. Request only reports which are needed and limit the contents to exactly the information required.

7. To avoid confusion, there should be some central record of places where specific reports have been sent.

8. Principals should handle all evaluations of teachers within their buildings. They may wish to consult with the director of special education.

9. Keep forms clear and easy to quickly decipher.

10. Give new teacher applicants a warm feeling about having contacted your school district.

Chapter 15

SUMMARY AND GENERAL GUIDELINES

BEING A DIRECTOR of special education is a most challenging and fulfilling role. The simulation exercises in this book are based on the experiences of the author while serving as a director of special education. Life in this role is never dull, as the variety of daily experiences is tremendous.

The material in this book will help the reader confront the various situations found in the real experience of being a director of special education.

To summarize, here are some guidelines which will help those persons in the position of director of special education.

1. Develop specific policies and procedures for the daily operation of the special education and special service programs.

2. Have systematic communication processes with all individuals and agencies concerned with the special education program, including, but not limited to: personnel, general education staff, parents and the news media.

3. Keep the superintendent well informed about special education and special services programs.

4. Know the total school system and community operations, including the master teacher contract provisions, line and staff relationships, power structures in both the school and community, local and state organizational patterns and other relevant information.

5. Join a coalition of directors of special education to develop regular communication patterns with your counterparts.

6. Periodically evaluate your functioning and your priorities.

7. Arrange for periodic evaluation of all special education and special service programs.

8. Have written individual educational plans and written program goals.

9. Correlate wherever possible the special education and general education programs.

10. Deal honestly with all people, especially parents.

11. If you do not know the answer, say so.

12. If you have delegated a responsibility to another, follow through in appropriate referrals.

13. Encourage leadership and growth of all of your staff, including both professional and nonprofessional personnel.

14. Be prompt in returning communications. Remember, silence is the highest form of scorn.

15. Uphold the dignity of all those with whom you relate.

16. Wherever possible, depend on personal face to face communications, and encourage your staff to do likewise.

17. Keep a well-balanced perspective of your role and see the humor in situations.

18. Remember, special education is not the answer to every problem.

19. Provide a follow up plan or referral for those individuals beyond school age who still require some intervention.

20. Make maximum use of all appropriate agencies in providing services to handicapped individuals.

21. Have faith in people and expect them to perform well.

22. View your program with pride and dissatisfaction, always seeking to improve the quality of good services.

23. Know your resources thoroughly, including both individuals and agencies.

24. Keep a goal directed positive attitude.

25. Keep as your highest priority the provision of the best quality programs and services for the handicapped.

And finally, if you feel that the success of the total special education program depends only on you, reevaluate your functioning and your perspective.

If you feel you have made all the positive contributions you can make in a particular school system, and will coast in the role from here on, slide out fast to another more challenging role, perhaps as director of special education in another school system.

Review these principles and guidelines periodically and add some of your own.

Best wishes and have fun in your role as director of special education.

INDEX

147944

DATE DUE

NO 24 '76			
UPI			Printed in USA